Amazing
Boats

by Frances Ridley

Contents

Words in **bold** are explained in the glossary.

Copyright © ticktock Entertainment Ltd 2008
First published in Great Britain in 2008 by ticktock Media Ltd.,
Unit 2, Orchard Business Centre, North Farm Road,
Tunbridge Wells, Kent, TN2 3XF

We would like to thank: Penny Worms, Alix Wood and the National Literacy Trust.

ISBN 978 1 84696 772 6

Printed in China

A CIP catalogue record for this book is available from the British Library.
Picture credits: b=bottom; c=centre; t=top; r=right; l=left
Alamy: 19t, 25t; Bethen of Cowes: 16-17; British Antarctic Survey: 12-13; Corbis: 2, 8-9c, 14-15, 17t, 18-19; Hawkes Ocean Technologies: 9t; John Clark Photography: 3, 4-5c; RNLI: 20-21; Stena: 22-23; ticktock Picture Archive: 5t, 6-7, back cover cl; World of Residence: 10-11, back cover cr; Yamaha: 23t.

Every effort has been made to trace the copyright holders, and we apologise in advance for any unintentional omissions. We would be pleased to insert the appropriate acknowledgements in any subsequent edition of this publication.

California Quake Drag Boat

Drag boats are fast racing boats.
They are more like rockets.
The California Quake can go
at 370 km/h.

The top of the Quake breaks free in a crash to keep the driver safe.

The driver's helmet is linked to an air bottle. They can breathe underwater if they have to.

Polaris Virage TX Jetski

Jetski riders surf across waves at high speed. A jetski can go at nearly 97 km/h! You steer it with handlebars – just like a bike.

Jetski riders can
do turns, jumps
and loops.
They can even
dive underwater!

The jetski stops if the rider
falls off so the rider can
get back on.

Deep Flight Submersible

A submersible is a boat that can go underwater. The Deep Flight is small – it only holds one person. It is used to explore the deep sea.

The Deep Flight has four cameras.
It has six lights because
it is totally dark in the
deep sea.

The World Luxury Liner

The passengers on The World aren't on holiday – they live there! They buy a set of rooms and then travel all over the planet.

The World's **hull** is made of huge pieces of steel.

The World has 12 **decks**. There are cinemas, restaurants, theatres and swimming pools!

James Clark Ross Research Ship

Research ships take scientists to explore different places. They can spend months at sea.

The James Clark Ross can smash through thick ice. It weighs 5,732 tonnes (that's more than 30 jumbo jets)! Its hull is made of strong steel.

The James Clark Ross is in Antarctica. The scientists on the ship find out about the sea and the weather.

Los Angeles Fireboats

Los Angeles is a big port in America. Its fireboats fight fires on ships and buildings by the sea.

Each boat
has six powerful pumps.
They suck in water and
fire it out of water-guns.
The guns shoot jets
of water as high as
150 metres.

Nimitz-Class Aircraft Carrier

The Nimitz-class aircraft carrier is a huge warship. It is as long as three football pitches.

The Nimitz carries 85 planes and six helicopters. Fuel for the planes and helicopters is kept in tanks the size of swimming pools!

It uses the latest computers and **radar**.

The Nimitz has over 6,000 crew!

Jahre Viking Oil Supertanker

Oil supertankers are the biggest ships in the world. The Jahre Viking's deck is as large as four football pitches.

The ship is so big that the crew use bikes to get around!

The Jahre Viking takes the oil to a **refinery**. It travels slowly – its top speed is 18 km/h.

Trent-Type Lifeboat

Lifeboats rescue people from the sea. They are strong boats with brave crews!

The Trent-Type Lifeboat can carry six crew and ten survivors.

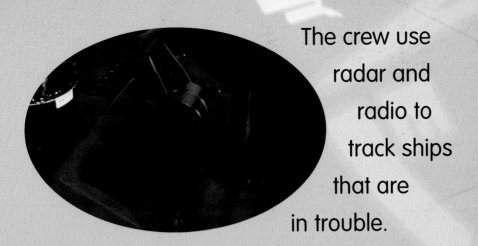

The crew use radar and radio to track ships that are in trouble.

Rescued people go to the survivors' **cabin**. The cabin has heaters, clothes, hot drinks and snacks.

Catamaran Ferries

Ferries carry passengers, cars and goods. Catamaran ferries have two hulls instead of one. The hulls cut through the waves, making the ride smoother and faster.

The four engines on the Stena Discovery are as powerful as 600 car engines!

It holds 200 cars and 1,000 passengers. It has bars and restaurants on board.

Glossary

cabin	A room on a ship.
deck	The floor of a ship.
hull	The bottom part of a ship – the part that floats on the water.
radar	A way to detect objects that are far away.
refinery	Where oil is turned into petrol.

Index